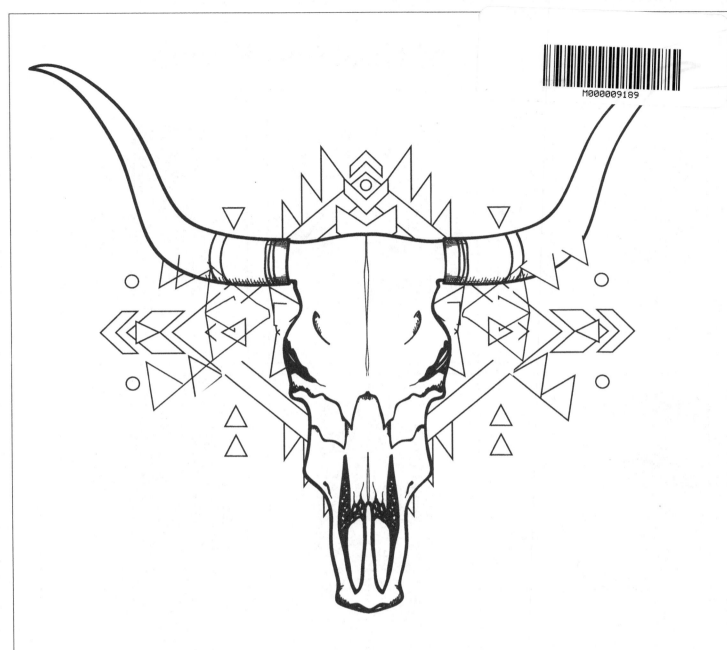

Coloring Book For Men

Anti-Stress Designs Vol 1

ART THERAPY COLORING

Preview of Coloring Pages

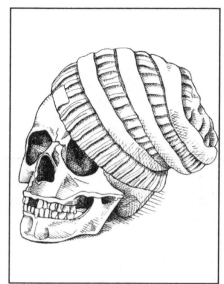

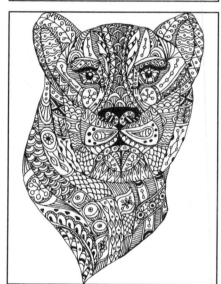

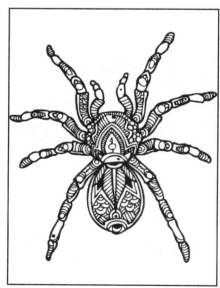

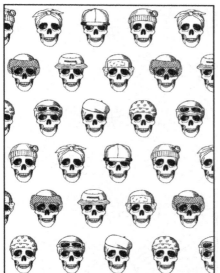

Did You Enjoy Our Coloring Book?

We Want To Hear About It!

Help spread the word about our adult coloring books! We give 10% of all proceeds from Art Therapy products to benefit pancreatic cancer patients and their families.

The best way to spread the word is through **Amazon reviews**. We know how busy you are, especially with all of that coloring, but we would appreciate it!

Visit our website at **www.arttherapycoloring.com**

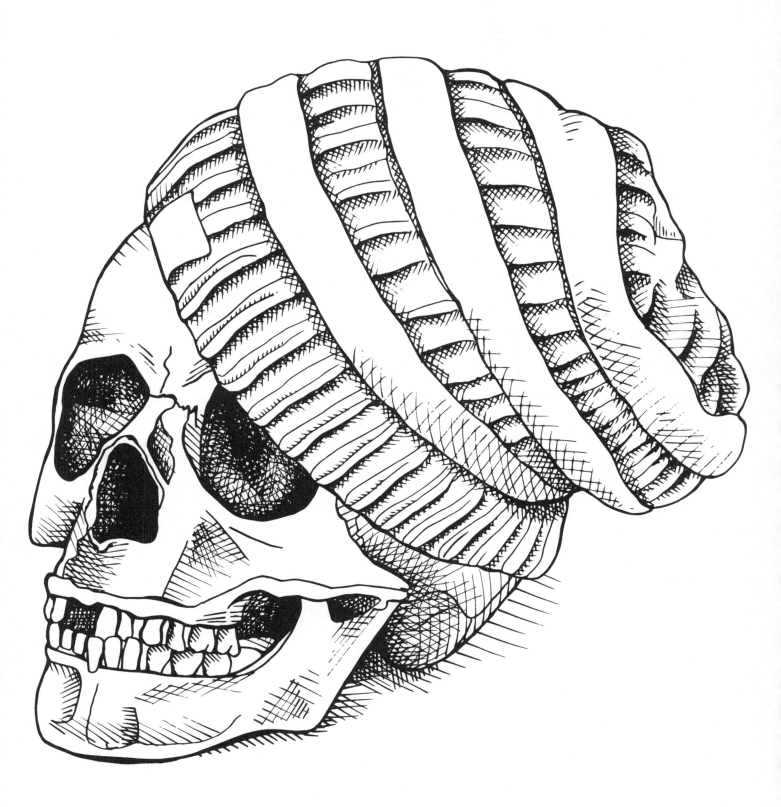

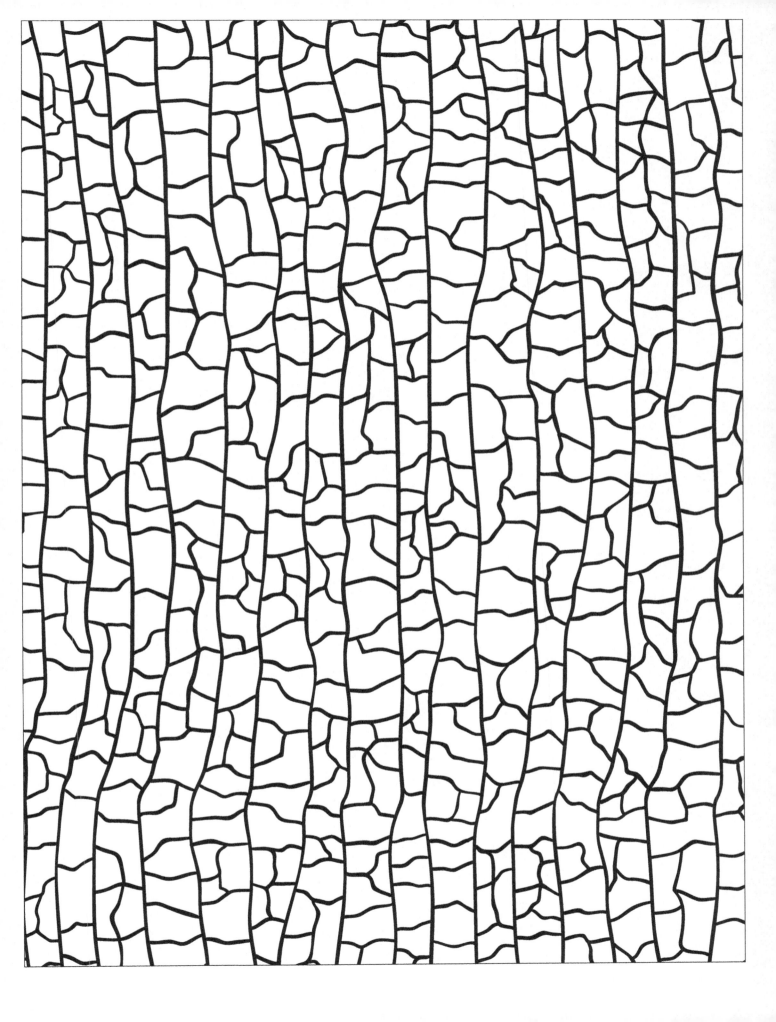

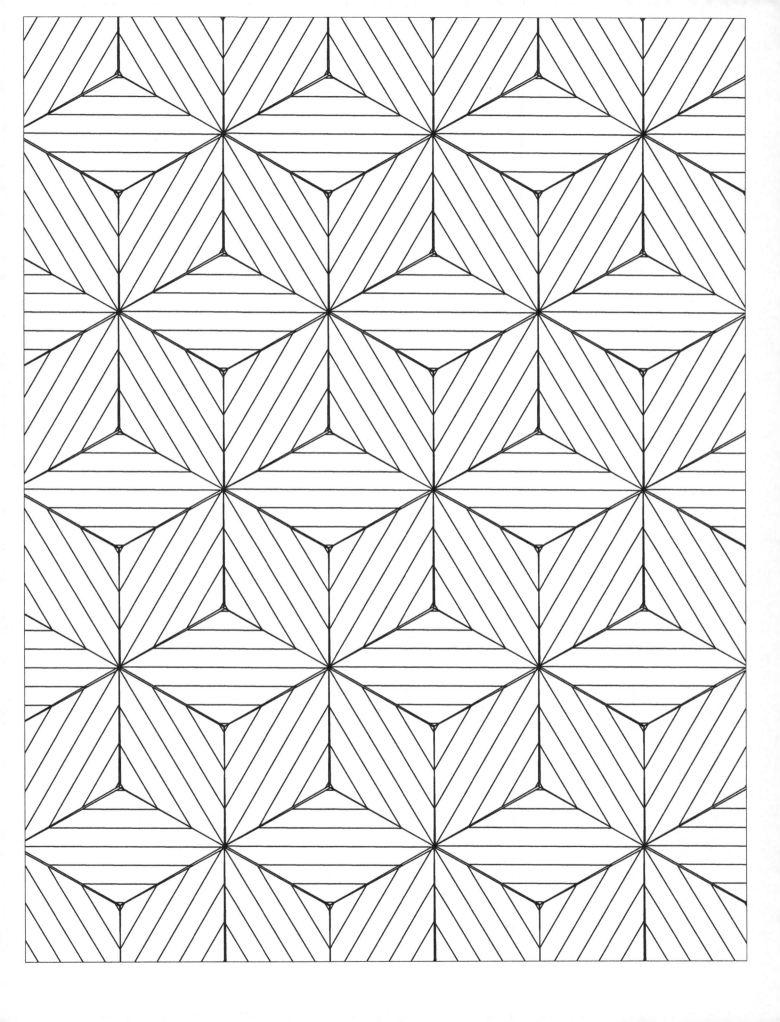

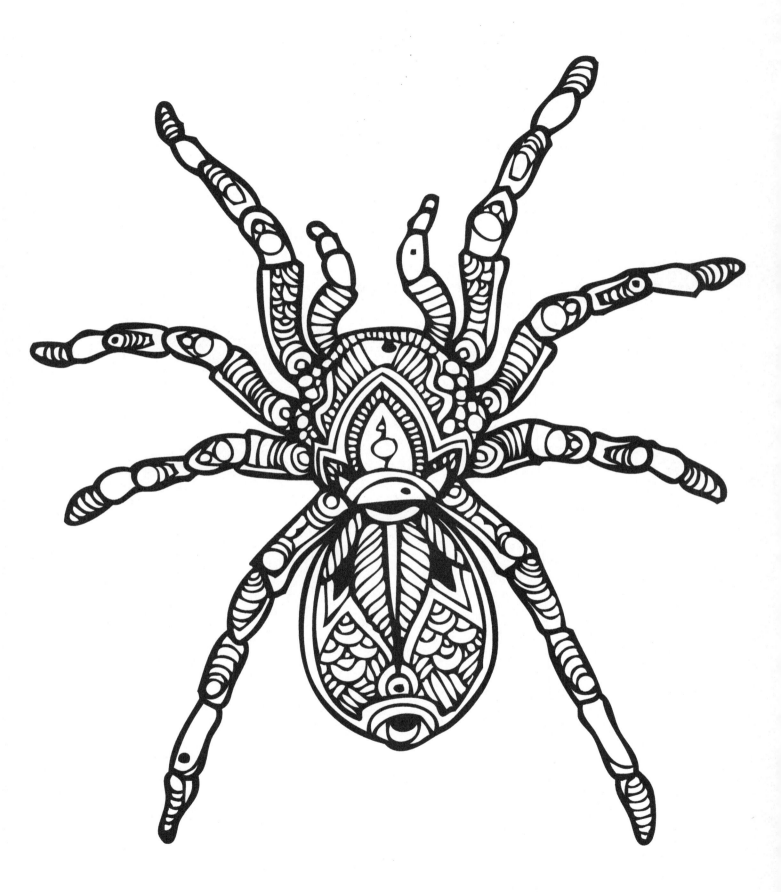

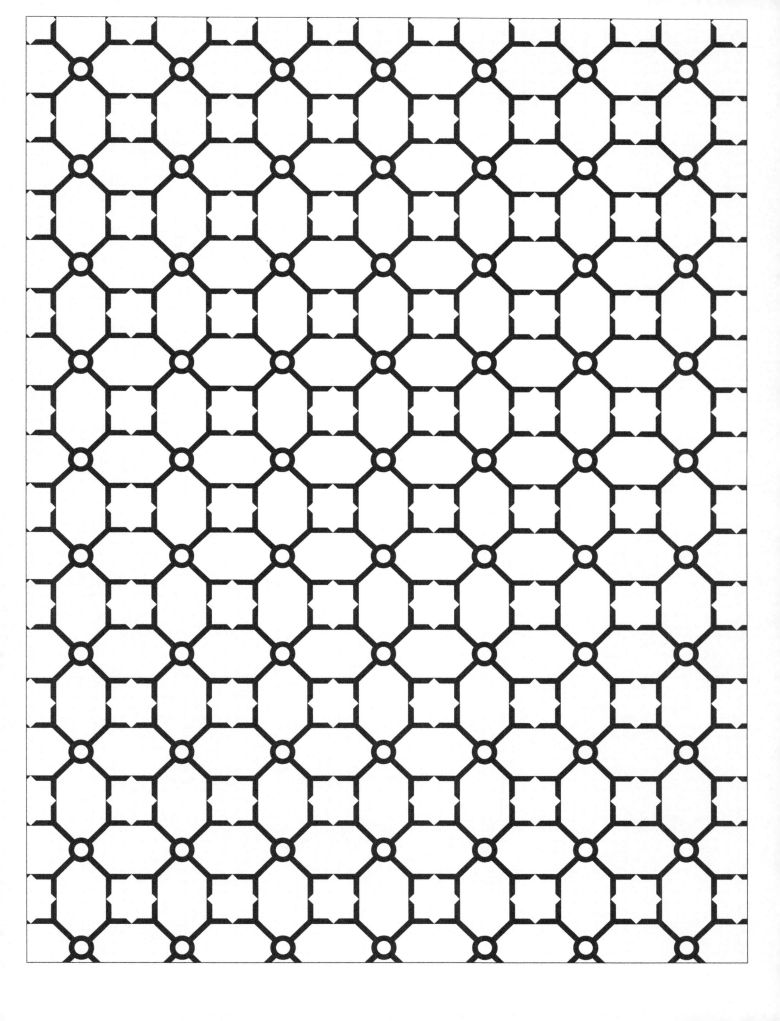

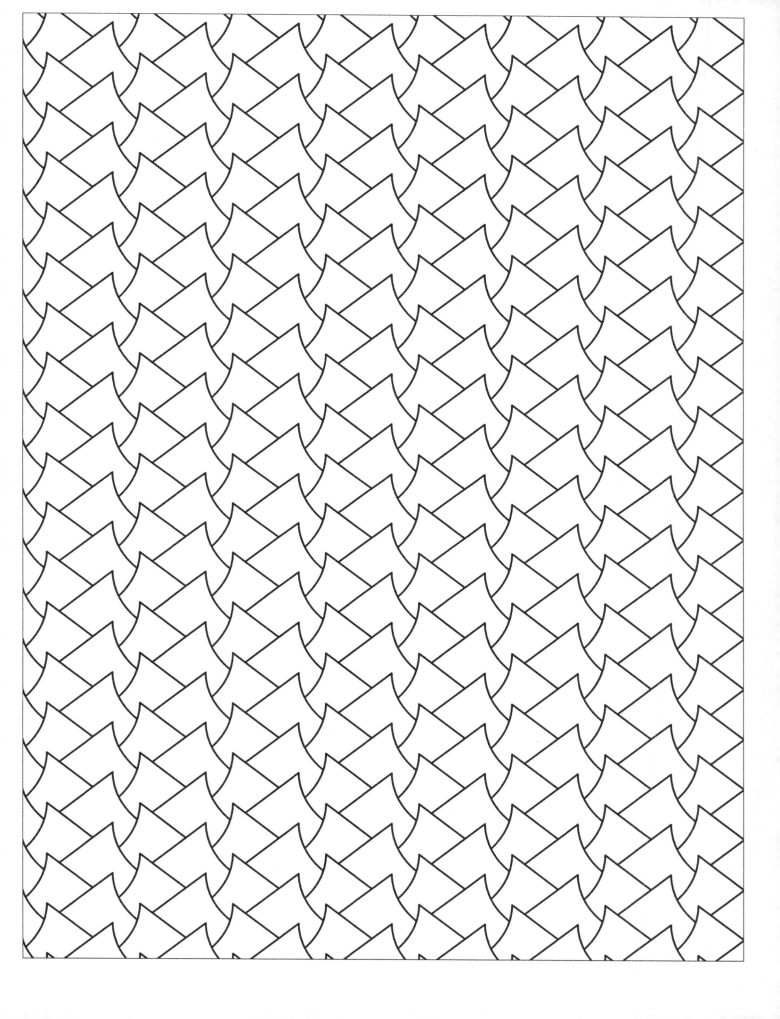

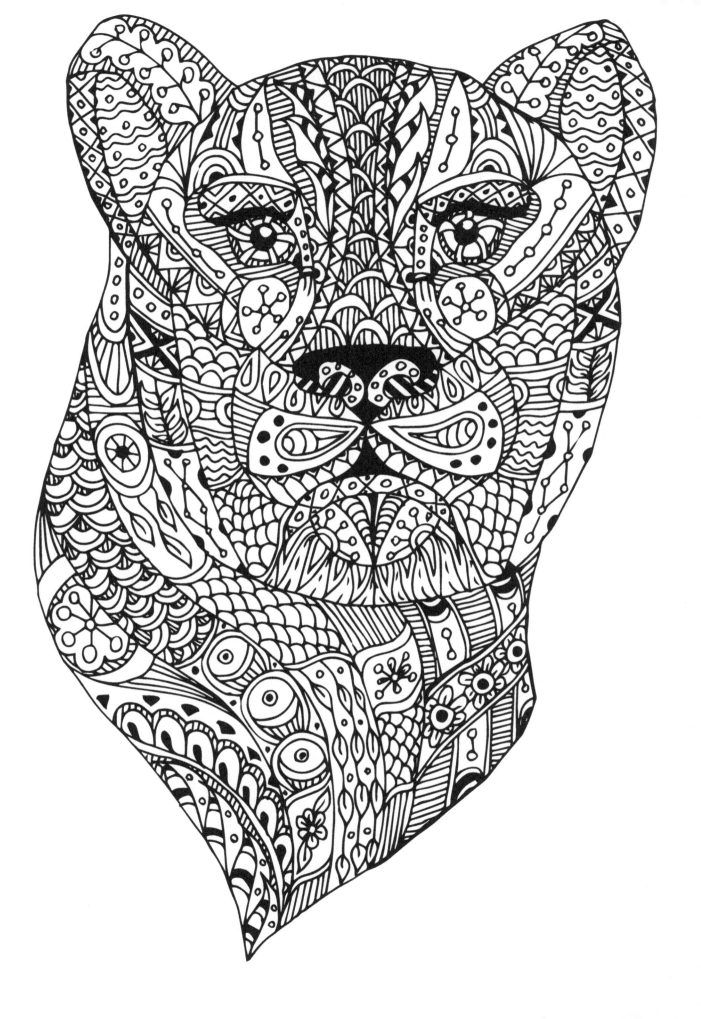

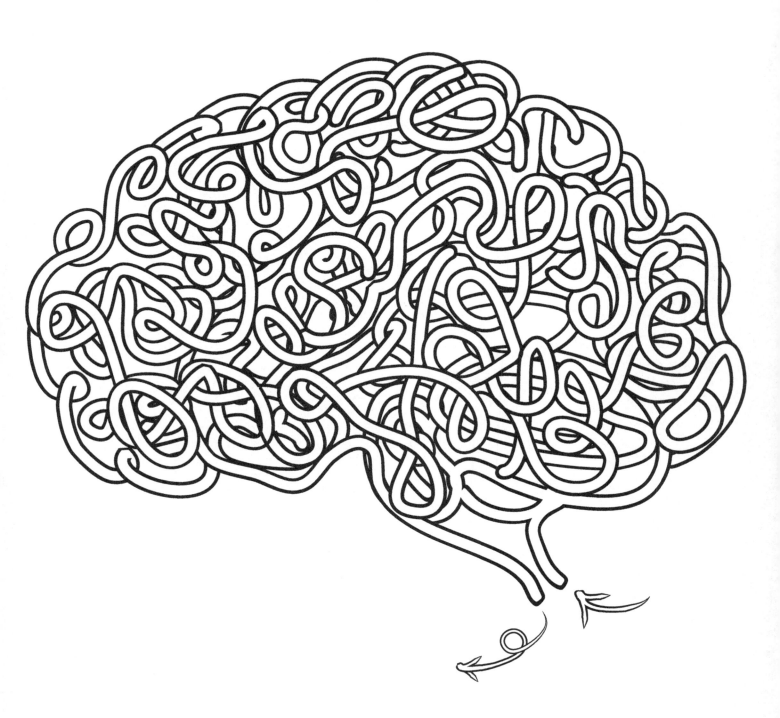

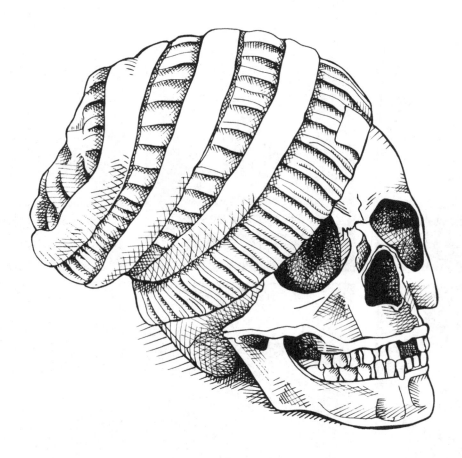

Black Background Coloring Books

BUTTERFLY
COLORING BOOK
FOR ADULTS
Black Background

BUTTERFLY
COLORING BOOK
FOR ADULTS VOL 2
Black Background

FLOWER
COLORING BOOK
FOR ADULTS
Black Background

ANIMAL
COLORING BOOK
FOR ADULTS
Black Background

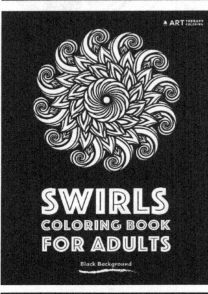

SWIRLS
COLORING BOOK
FOR ADULTS
Black Background

PATTERNS
COLORING BOOK
FOR ADULTS
Black Background

MANDALA
COLORING BOOK
FOR SENIORS
Black Background

BUTTERFLY
COLORING BOOK
FOR SENIORS
Black Background

CHRISTMAS
COLORING BOOK
FOR SENIORS
Black Background

Black Background Coloring Books

CHRISTMAS
COLORING BOOK
FOR ADULTS
Black Background

FESTIVE ANIMAL
CHRISTMAS
COLORING BOOK FOR ADULTS
Black Background

MERRY CHRISTMAS
AND HAPPY NEW YEAR

CHRISTMAS
COLORING BOOK
FOR TEENS
Black Background

MERMAID
COLORING BOOK
FOR TEENS
Black Background

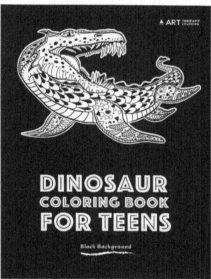

DINOSAUR
COLORING BOOK
FOR TEENS
Black Background

SKULL
COLORING BOOK
FOR TEENS
Black Background

MOTORCYCLE
COLORING BOOK
FOR TEENS
Black Background

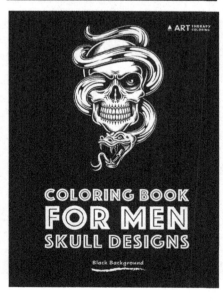

COLORING BOOK
FOR MEN
SKULL DESIGNS
Black Background

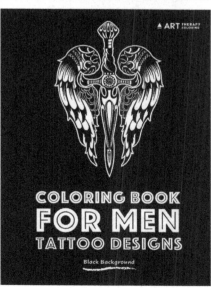

COLORING BOOK
FOR MEN
TATTOO DESIGNS
Black Background

www.arttherapycoloring.com

BUTTERFLY COLORING BOOK FOR ADULTS

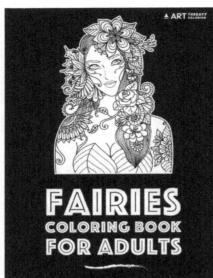

FAIRIES COLORING BOOK FOR ADULTS

MERMAID COLORING BOOK FOR ADULTS

INTRICATE COLORING BOOK FOR ADULTS VOL 1

INTRICATE COLORING BOOK FOR ADULTS VOL 2

INTRICATE COLORING BOOK FOR ADULTS VOL 3

ANIMAL COLORING BOOK FOR ADULTS VOL 1

ANIMAL COLORING BOOK FOR ADULTS VOL 2

ANIMAL COLORING BOOK FOR ADULTS VOL 3

Art Therapy Coloring Books For Men

Coloring Book For Men

Anti-Stress Designs Vol 1

ART THERAPY COLORING

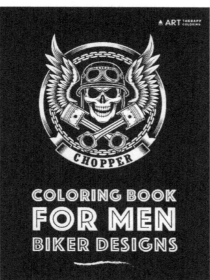

CHOPPER

COLORING BOOK
FOR MEN
BIKER DESIGNS

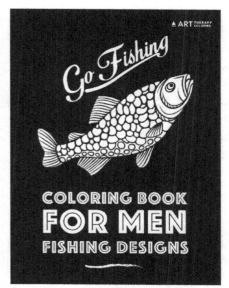

Go Fishing

COLORING BOOK
FOR MEN
FISHING DESIGNS

NATURE
COLORING BOOK
FOR SENIORS MEN

ANIMAL
COLORING BOOK
FOR SENIORS MEN

OCEAN
COLORING BOOK
FOR SENIORS MEN

WISH·YOU·WERE·BEER

COLORING BOOK
FOR MEN
BEER DESIGNS

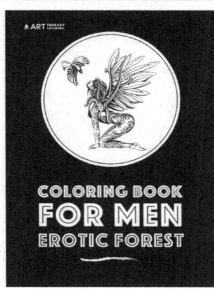

COLORING BOOK
FOR MEN
EROTIC FOREST

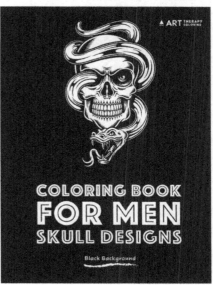

COLORING BOOK
FOR MEN
SKULL DESIGNS

Black Background

CAT & COFFEE COLORING BOOK FOR ADULTS

DOG & COFFEE COLORING BOOK FOR ADULTS

BIRD COLORING BOOK FOR ADULTS VOL 1

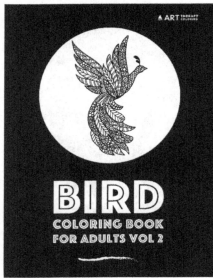

BIRD COLORING BOOK FOR ADULTS VOL 2

INTRICATE COLORING BOOK FOR ADULTS VOL 4

INTRICATE COLORING BOOK FOR ADULTS VOL 5

INTRICATE COLORING BOOK FOR ADULTS VOL 6

ANIMAL COLORING BOOK FOR ADULTS VOL 5

ANIMAL COLORING BOOK FOR ADULTS VOL 6

Art Therapy Adult Coloring Books

FLOWER
COLORING BOOK
FOR ADULTS VOL 1

FLOWER
COLORING BOOK
FOR ADULTS VOL 2

FLOWER
COLORING BOOK
FOR ADULTS VOL 3

FLOWER
COLORING BOOK
FOR ADULTS VOL 4

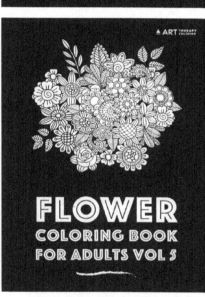

FLOWER
COLORING BOOK
FOR ADULTS VOL 5

FLOWER
COLORING BOOK
FOR ADULTS VOL 6

ANIMAL
COLORING BOOK
FOR ADULTS VOL 4

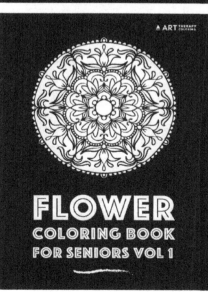

FLOWER
COLORING BOOK
FOR SENIORS VOL 1

FLOWER
COLORING BOOK
FOR SENIORS VOL 2

www.arttherapycoloring.com

CHRISTMAS
COLORING BOOK
FOR ADULTS VOL 2

CHRISTMAS
COLORING BOOK
FOR ADULTS VOL 3

MANDALA
COLORING BOOK
FOR SENIORS

ANIMAL
COLORING BOOK
FOR TEENS VOL 1

ANIMAL
COLORING BOOK
FOR TEENS VOL 2

BUTTERFLY
COLORING BOOK
FOR TEENS

GEOMETRIC
COLORING BOOK
FOR TEENS

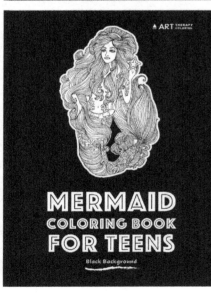

MERMAID
COLORING BOOK
FOR TEENS
Black Background

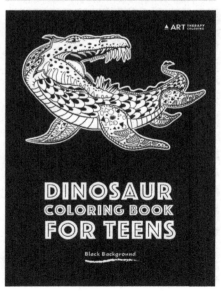

DINOSAUR
COLORING BOOK
FOR TEENS
Black Background

Art Therapy Coloring Books For Teens

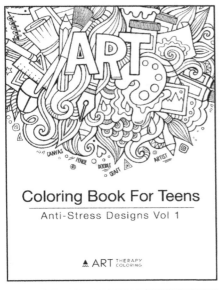

Coloring Book For Teens
Anti-Stress Designs Vol 1

▲ ART THERAPY COLORING

Coloring Book For Teens
Anti-Stress Designs Vol 2

▲ ART THERAPY COLORING

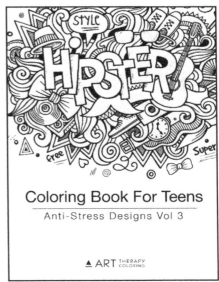

Coloring Book For Teens
Anti-Stress Designs Vol 3

▲ ART THERAPY COLORING

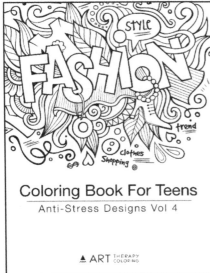

Coloring Book For Teens
Anti-Stress Designs Vol 4

▲ ART THERAPY COLORING

Coloring Book For Teens
Anti-Stress Designs Vol 5

▲ ART THERAPY COLORING

Coloring Book For Teens
Anti-Stress Designs Vol 6

▲ ART THERAPY COLORING

Coloring Book For Teens
Anti-Stress Designs Vol 7

▲ ART THERAPY COLORING

Coloring Book For Teens
Anti-Stress Designs Vol 8

▲ ART THERAPY COLORING

www.arttherapycoloring.com

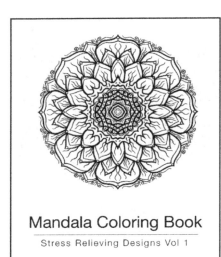

Mandala Coloring Book

Stress Relieving Designs Vol 1

▲ ART THERAPY COLORING

Anti-Stress Coloring Book

Stress Relieving Designs Vol 1

▲ ART THERAPY COLORING

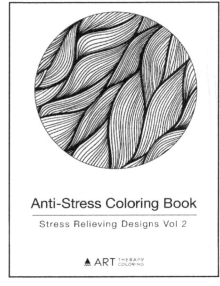

Anti-Stress Coloring Book

Stress Relieving Designs Vol 2

▲ ART THERAPY COLORING

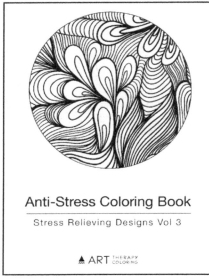

Anti-Stress Coloring Book

Stress Relieving Designs Vol 3

▲ ART THERAPY COLORING

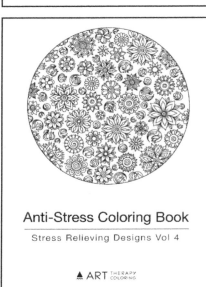

Anti-Stress Coloring Book

Stress Relieving Designs Vol 4

▲ ART THERAPY COLORING

Coloring Book For Seniors

Nature Designs Vol 2

▲ ART THERAPY COLORING

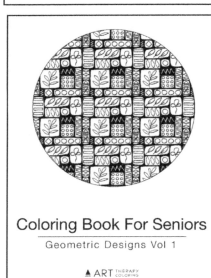

Coloring Book For Seniors

Geometric Designs Vol 1

▲ ART THERAPY COLORING

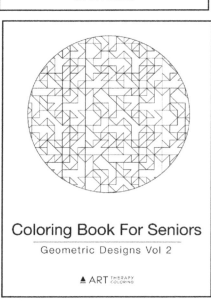

Coloring Book For Seniors

Geometric Designs Vol 2

▲ ART THERAPY COLORING

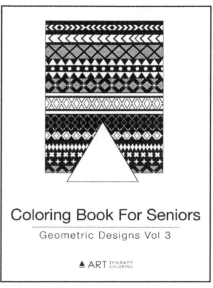

Coloring Book For Seniors

Geometric Designs Vol 3

▲ ART THERAPY COLORING

Art Therapy Coloring Books For Seniors

Coloring Book For Seniors
Anti-Stress Designs Vol 1

▲ ART THERAPY COLORING

Coloring Book For Seniors
Anti-Stress Designs Vol 2

▲ ART THERAPY COLORING

Coloring Book For Seniors
Anti-Stress Designs Vol 3

▲ ART THERAPY COLORING

Coloring Book For Seniors
Anti-Stress Designs Vol 4

▲ ART THERAPY COLORING

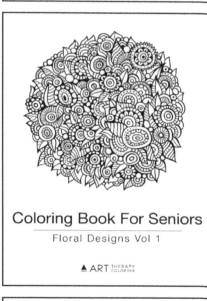

Coloring Book For Seniors
Floral Designs Vol 1

▲ ART THERAPY COLORING

Coloring Book For Seniors
Floral Designs Vol 2

▲ ART THERAPY COLORING

Coloring Book For Seniors
Nature Designs Vol 1

▲ ART THERAPY COLORING

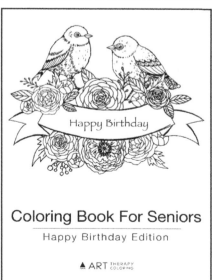

Coloring Book For Seniors
Happy Birthday Edition

▲ ART THERAPY COLORING

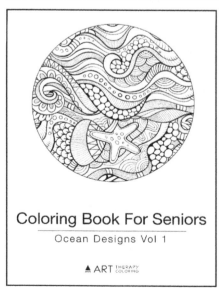

Coloring Book For Seniors
Ocean Designs Vol 1

▲ ART THERAPY COLORING

www.arttherapycoloring.com

Anti-Stress Coloring Book
Floral Designs Vol 1

ART THERAPY COLORING

Anti-Stress Coloring Book
Floral Designs Vol 2

ART THERAPY COLORING

Anti-Stress Coloring Book
Nature Designs Vol 1

ART THERAPY COLORING

Anti-Stress Coloring Book
Nature Designs Vol 2

ART THERAPY COLORING

Anti-Stress Coloring Book
Nature Designs Vol 3

ART THERAPY COLORING

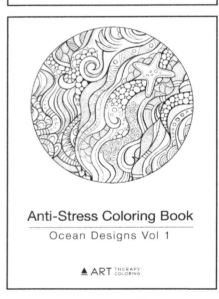

Anti-Stress Coloring Book
Ocean Designs Vol 1

ART THERAPY COLORING

Anti-Stress Coloring Book
Owl Designs Vol 1

ART THERAPY COLORING

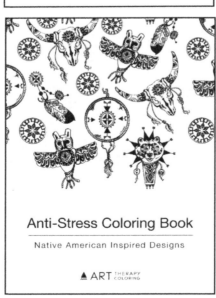

Anti-Stress Coloring Book
Native American Inspired Designs

ART THERAPY COLORING

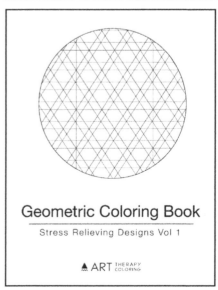

Geometric Coloring Book
Stress Relieving Designs Vol 1

ART THERAPY COLORING

Art Therapy Adult Coloring Books

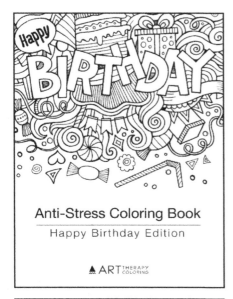

Anti-Stress Coloring Book

Happy Birthday Edition

▲ ART THERAPY COLORING

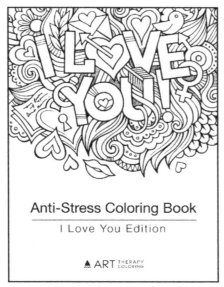

Anti-Stress Coloring Book

I Love You Edition

▲ ART THERAPY COLORING

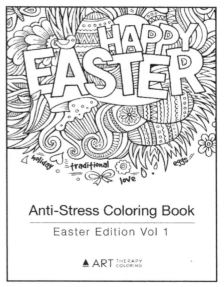

Anti-Stress Coloring Book

Easter Edition Vol 1

▲ ART THERAPY COLORING

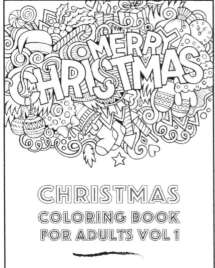

CHRISTMAS
COLORING BOOK
FOR ADULTS VOL 1

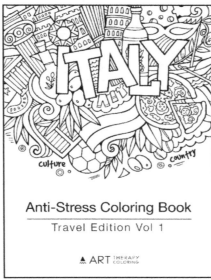

Anti-Stress Coloring Book

Travel Edition Vol 1

▲ ART THERAPY COLORING

Anti-Stress Coloring Book

The Four Seasons Edition

▲ ART THERAPY COLORING

Anti-Stress Coloring Book

Mother's Day Edition

▲ ART THERAPY COLORING

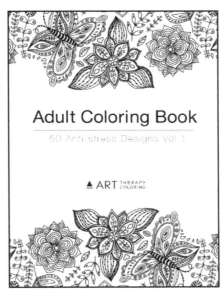

Adult Coloring Book

50 Anti-stress Designs Vol 1

▲ ART THERAPY COLORING

Coloring Book For Men
Anti-Stress Designs Vol 1

Copyright © 2015 by Art Therapy Coloring
All Rights Reserved

Published by:
Art Therapy Coloring
El Dorado Hills, California
www.arttherapycoloring.com

ISBN: 978-1-944427-24-5